"To die, to sleep;
To sleep: perchance to dream: ay, there's the rub;
For in that sleep of death what dreams may come."

~William Shakespeare
(Hamlet - Act III, Scene I, Line 77)

Also by Carly Herriges

Good Advice from Bad Women
(Silver Bow Publishing)

Grief is a Circle

by

Carly Herriges

720 – Sixth Street, Box # 5
New Westminster, BC
V3C 3C5   CANADA

Title: Grief is a Circle
Author: Carly Herriges
Publisher: Silver Bow Publishing
Cover Design: "The Parrot and the Mulberry Tree" painting by Candice James
Layout and Editing: Candice James

All rights reserved including the right to reproduce or translate this book or any portions thereof, in any form without the permission of the publisher. Except for the use of short passages for review purposes, no part of this book may be reproduced, in part or in whole, or transmitted in any form or by any means, electronically or mechanically, including photocopying, recording, or any information or storage retrieval system without prior permission in writing from the publisher or a licence from the Canadian Copyright Collective Agency (Access Copyright).

www.silverbowpublishing.com
info@silverbowpublishing.com
© silver bow publishing 2022
ISBN: 9781774032114 (print)
ISBN: 9781774032121 (eBook)

Library and Archives Canada Cataloguing in Publication

Title: Grief is a circle / Carly Herriges.
Names: Herriges, Carly, 1994- author.
Description: Poems.
Identifiers: Canadiana (print) 20220247218 | Canadiana (ebook) 20220247269 | ISBN 9781774032114
   (softcover) | ISBN 9781774032121 (EPUB)
Classification: LCC PS3608.E77 G75 2022 | DDC 811/.6—dc23

For Mom and Dad,
who showed me how to find beauty
in the messiness of this life.

FOREWORD

This poetry collection is an exploration of grief, life, love and fear. I've found that, for me, the fear of violence goes hand in hand with what I know about moving through life and informs the way I know to grieve. The poems in this collection came together in a mess of words that I found myself trying to untangle, without making progress. What it taught me most is that grief is wholly individual, there isn't a simple guidebook to follow to make it through.

My previous collection, Good Advice From Bad Women was published in 2019 and I am incredibly proud of it. Writing is a constant in my life that I rely on to help keep me afloat when life becomes too much, as it did in March of 2020. I am always trying to learn and grow my craft as much as I can, to become not only a better writer technically, but a better storyteller. I hope to write work that touches people and helps them discover new things about themselves and about the world.

I have been referring to this collection as 'Grief is a Circle', something I was told by a friend. There is no end to the grieving process, losing someone you love leaves a space in your life that cannot be filled. There is no right time to "get over it" or "move on". Ultimately, you live day by day and hope that you give yourself enough space to get through the hard days. This collection is compiled of hard days, of easy days and the days in between. I hope that this work reflects the messiness of grief, and ultimately the beauty of what it is to truly know yourself.

Table of Contents

P.S. ... 11
Cast of Characters ... 12
A Fear that Starts with Breakfast ... 14
We were all trying so hard to be grown ,,, 17
The Monster Under the Bed ... 19
The Men are Always Teaching ... 21
The Party ... 22
The Killer is a Father Too ... 24
      (After Olivia Gatwood)
Girl Talk ... 27
She Never Returned ... 30
Alternate Heaven for Femicide Victims ... 31
A Fear By any Other Name ... 32
The Men are Always Watching ... 33
Habit ... 34
Things I Learned About Myself ... 36
The Men are Always Talking ... 38
So Maybe My Room is a Mess ... 39
The Ways Fear Builds a Home In a Body ,,, 40
Been Found Poem ... 41
The Men are Always Helping ... 42
Tangled ... 44
The Unsub ... 46
An Interlude for My Mother ...
      Who Wishes I'd Watch More Comedies ... 53
Things I Know from Spending
      Most of My Life Around Women ... 54
The Grief and the Promises ... 56
First Timer ... 58
All the Bars are Funeral Homes ... 60
For Wanda and the Hex ... 61
Elegy ... 64
I Grieve the Girl I Would Have Been ... 65
Things I Should Have Said at the Funeral and After ... 66
The Sun Mourns Icarus ... 71
The Gum Tree ... 73
When the Marvel Women Have Dinner ... 75
An October Afternoon ... 76

The Moon and the Sea ... 77
Living Deadly ... 79
Men Who Have Held Me ... 81
Don't You Have a Bed Partner? ... 83
The first girl I loved, ... 85
Moonsong ... 86
The Ways I've Loved You ... 87
Girls Like Me Don't Know How to be Quiet ... 88
Summer ... 89
If I were a God, ... 90
I Don't Remember My Teen Years ... 91
New Vocabulary ... 93
Persephone ... 95
An Ode to Things that Make Me Proud to be Fat ... 97
P.S. ... 99

Author Profile ... 101

P.S.

I don't remember the exact day, maybe it was Spring.
In my early twenties I realized I had no idea how to grieve.
I knew what everyone said, I could tell you the five stages,
I could point you to all the books,
I could recite song lyrics and words of poets.
But, in practice, I didn't know where to start.
What I did know was that death was something
I had grown accustomed to.
There was a joke we would make in high school,
that before the end of the year, someone would be pregnant,
and someone would be dead.

As dark as that sounds, it was entirely normal.
We'd been burying our schoolmates for years at that point.
And, for an abstinence only teaching school district,
teen pregnancy wasn't a new concept either.
What I knew about grief however, was that it makes people quiet.
They isolate themselves into their own corners and don't come out.
Until one day, maybe in the Spring, there they are,
smiling in their bathing suits, ready to carry on their lives.

The work you are going to read is an exploration, maybe a map,
maybe a shout into the void. It is a collection of the things I know
about death, grief, life and love, all of which are a jumbled mess
of emotions I am constantly trying to untangle.
In the pages ahead of you, you will meet many people,
some from my life, some from the news, and some
from the thing I surround myself with most, television.

I hope that these small pieces of myself give you some understanding
of how messy grief really is, how you cannot have grief without death,
and how you often cannot have death without fear.
All of these things informed the book ahead of you and informed me
on how to best move through the world
when you have no corner to isolate yourself in.

Cast of Characters

Narrator- As storyteller, sometimes unreliable, often afraid, angry or embarrassed.

Mother- As the vein you come from, who knows you better than yourself, salt you would have added to the sauce but you tasted it and decided it is best left alone.

Father- As the best man Narrator knows, a fear you feel even when you do not want to, your favorite Christmas present to shop for, the person I call when everything falls apart.

Sisters- As your mirror and your measuring tape, that which looks like you and through you, the only people you fight with as much as you laugh with.

Aunts- As something that is in front of you one moment and gone the next, a hummingbird, a bumble bee, a way to say 'I would die for you even though I did not raise you'.

Man- As the thing I fear most in the dark, paranoia, the place where no light enters.

Her- As the lover, the moon and sun, the feeling when you leave a movie in the middle of the day, the heat that comes off the parking lot.

The Desert- As a place that takes our bodies, an oppressive heat, the hand on your hip you did not ask for, but also, the place where the sky breaks open during the longest week in June, a flower growing through the sidewalk, the person you want to hug after a long day.

The Gods- As an envy and admiration, that which you build an altar for and also sing drunk karaoke with, the thing inside of you and outside of you at once.

The Unsub-   As the reason I stay up staring at the door,
check the locks on the windows once, twice, three
times. The BPM when you startle awake at the sound
of the air conditioning turning on in the middle
of the night, willing to sweat in the dark
in order to sleep through the night.

A Fear that Starts with Breakfast

I have slept late into the afternoon,
my parents are running errands,
and I am lying on the couch with my sister.
The television is playing something we've seen before.
I am eating lunch that I have called breakfast,
still in my pajamas,
my skin smells like sleep.

When they enter,
the air around them is charged,
there is already something they haven't said.
So it's like this,
we got the call this morning,
it happened so fast,
she ended it and he was so angry,
she ended it and he was so heartbroken,
she ended it and he said he loved her.
He ended them both,
if he couldn't have her,
no one would,
not even us,
not ever.

And I am three weeks past my 16th birthday,
I have been handed this fear,
as clean and plump as a newborn baby.
I have to take a shower,
I have to wash my hair,
I have to cry where no one can see.
I do not sleep,
I stare at the ceiling,
and fantasize it collapsing onto me,
imagine my bedside lamp a blazing inferno.
The dinner we reluctantly cooked,
poison churning in my gut.
Because if this is true,
then everything I trust must be a weapon.

He loved her,
so he ended them both,
he loved her,
he loved,
loved.

I am three weeks past 16,
and have been given this new truth.
That someday,
someone you love,
someone who loves you,
will end you,
will own you so entirely,
they cut themselves open for it.
The fear is grown now,
a child I feed and tuck into bed,
as long as it is just us two,
I can keep us both safe.

I am sorry they made your body a warzone,
I am sorry they used your burial shroud as their white flag.

We were all trying so hard to be grown,

in our denim skirts and sandals,
our hair pushed away from our faces,
like we saw the city girls do on TV.
But we were still just kids;
still dependents,
on our parents,
and our siblings,
and each other.

We all thought we were so grown,
gossiping about how one of us,
lost our virginity to a football player,
and what it would be like to go to prom.

How we looked at each other
like fractured mirrors,
instead of stained glass windows.
We only saw the broken,
not the beautiful.

But we were still just kids,
still couldn't drive,
or buy our own tampons,
still kissing our father's cheeks,
still having nightmares of monsters
under our beds.

We didn't know that we weren't ready to grow up.
Didn't know what life would look like
when it wasn't drenched in the glow of youth.
not until showing up at school,
not until between first and second period,
not until the whispers.
Did you hear?
Can you believe it?
She was one of us.
A kid just trying to be grown.

In the picture on her profile
she had long winged liner,
but the one on the news
showed a bare face,
a full cheeked smile.

She was just like us.
Stuck in limbo between,
"stay a kid as long as you can",
and "act your age".
She was just like us,
until she wasn't.
Until the fight with her step-brother
got out of hand,
until whatever was said or unsaid
rang through the air like a bullet,
until she screamed or didn't.
until he cried or didn't.

She was just like us until she wasn't.
Because suddenly,
we were all so grown;
and she never would be.

The Monster Under the Bed

I want to tell you about the men that I know.
The good men.
The good men who raised me,
the good men I have raised.
The good men who have loved me,
the good men I have loved.
I want to tell you all about them,
about their laughs,
their hands,
the soft sweep of their hair.

But when I open my mouth to tell you about the good men,
the bad men crawl their way out,
they stick to my throat like black tar,
and their voices are the mindless drone of hornets
waiting above the water.
And now I am only telling you about the bad men,
who hold my dreams hostage,
whose invisible hands are always touching me,
always touching all of us with their dirty fingertips.

And now I am telling you about the women I know.
the good women,
who were raped by the bad men.
the crescent shaped bite marks
that sit on the skin and never fade.
The young girls with flat chests,
but bellies full of bad men.

And now I am telling you about the girl
they found in the desert.
And now I am telling you about the bad man,
who wore the mask of a good man.
Who raised smaller, younger men.
And those smaller, younger men were good men,
who loved the girl in the desert,
and also loved the man who left her there.

And now I am telling you about all of the good men,
how easily they could be bad men wearing masks,
and how all of the girls could easily be desert girls,
left smudged and smeared and only remembered,
for the bad men who left them there.

And now I can tell you how all of the good men.
Who are not bad men wearing masks.
How all of the good men,
who never become bad men,
can never outrun the memory the bad men leave.
How the good men can scrub and scrub and scrub the women,
but the women will never be clean.

How the bad men are grease covering an engine,
the more we have to fix them,
the dirtier we all become.

The Men are Always Teaching

When the man pretends to drug my drink,
he tells me it is for my own good.
Scolds my wandering eyes,
my small talk,
my too loud laugh.

Says I am lucky he is here to protect me,
lucky he is here to teach me.

I am seventeen minutes past the legal drinking age,
and I have already learned so much.

I should be thanking him really.
I heard a rumor that later
he had drugged another girl for real.

I wonder if he scolded her,
I wonder if he laughed at her.
I wonder if he made her say thank you.

The Party

Maybe it began in her feet.
The slap of her sandals hitting the sticky floor.
She can feel the beat of the music in the soles of her feet.
When the first man touched her without her permission,
when she shrugged it off with the flip of her hair.
When the third man touched her without her permission,
she shoved him so hard he spilled his drink.
Maybe it began in her throat,
the date rape drug swirling in with her ice and vodka.
Maybe it began in her stomach,
the way it churned like her body knew it was wrong.
Maybe it began in her scalp,
when she walked to meet her car in the parking lot,
and a hand reached out and grabbed her by her hair.
When she screamed and struggled and tried to push him away,
but found no strength in her arms.
Maybe it began in her arms,
in the way he held them down,
so he could fit both of her slim wrists in one hand.
Maybe it began in her knees,
how they struggled and fought to squirm her hips away from his.
More likely it began in the desert,
where the hiker mistook her yellow hair for brush.
More likely it began at the police station.
Some rookie cop being sent out to investigate a body.
He brought news cameras and came up with a name for the killer.
The Highway 10 Strangler.
The Desert Rapist.
The Date Rape Killer.
More likely it began at a birthday party,
the first boy/girl party she went to at 11.
The first time she knew the rules to the game
Seven Minutes in Heaven.
The first she discovered her body was not her property
but her currency.
When she didn't want to kiss her best friend
but he didn't want to be called a pussy,

so she took her clear lip gloss out of her pocket,
and smeared it across both of their mouths.
A bubblegum scented wound.
And all of their classmates oohed and aahed,
satisfied with the showmanship.
But it doesn't matter how it began,
the partygoers are tired now.
No one has found the cleverly named
strangler
rapist
killer.
It came out on the news that she had
smoked weed
engaged in sex
partook in under- age drinking once at a frat party.
The hiker whose name was in the article
is going to be on 60 Minutes next week.
The rookie cop was awarded
with a promotion to detective.
The journalist has found a new story,
of a new unnamed girl,
and her cleverly named
strangler
rapist
killer.

But who will pick up all of our red cups?
Who will sweep up the floor?
Who will turn off the music?
Who will be left to say her name?

The Killer is a Father Too
(after Olivia Gatwood)

There is a fear in my chest,
hearing about the men who laugh,
while the women struggle to breathe.
I see in my mind a photo of my father,
young and blonde haired,
before my mother,
before his serious job.
His limbs are long and lanky,
he has never held a baby,
has never put something small and fragile,
between his palms,
been responsible for not squeezing its head between them,
and crushing it like a grape.
Why does this remind me of my father?
Why does it make me fear him?

It is at this point, reader, that I am compelled to tell you,
my father is a good man,
he was a good man then,
he grew into a good husband,
a good father,
a good grandfather.
I say all of this in the hopes,
that you do not fear him,

I have just always been afraid of men,
and their potential to become beasts.
This lanky teen image of my father,
that makes me afraid is an alternate version of him.
The version that took a different road,
who tasted blood the first time
he was punched by his brother,
and never rid himself of the craving for more.
But in truth,
my father is the same man who,
when playing mermaids with his children,

in the pool at the height of July,
scooped a bee out of the water,
placed it in a spot of sun,
and made us watch until it flew away.

The same man who risked being stung,
to show his small and fragile daughters
that his hands
would not be a cemetery
for small and fragile things.

How tiring it is, to say "he killed her".
and the reply is not "who"
but instead, "which one?"

Girl Talk

There is a ritual to this,

the daisy chain around our chalk outlines.
We gloss our lips for this,

make our hair shiny for this,
empty and empty and empty ourselves for this.

While my sister makes dinner,
she is listening to the story of another murdered girl,

another body hallowed out by a hungry man,
gristle in his teeth.

She seasons the chicken cutlets,

as the narrator details
the monster dissecting someone who could be her.

This is girl talk.

While I braid Maria's hair,
I detail the smell of the man's cologne,

the way he shook my hand,
after he dumped the girl on the desert floor.

I howl like a coyote,
scream at the moon like a hawk in flight.

This is girl talk.

My mother sees my bookshelf as a cemetery,
the stories I collect of dead girls,

The way I look into them like mirrors.
She begs of me,

Please,
baby,
something sweeter.
It will taste better,
on the tongue.
Will rest easier on your pillow,
please,
baby,
something softer,
wrap yourself in something comfortable.
But this is girl talk.

This is our animal instinct at work.
We gather these bodies,
like fruit in our arms.

Collect them like mushrooms for our dinner,
fill and fill and fill ourselves with their stories.
bond over the ways we have escaped hungry men.

All of our girl talk,
all of our useless drivel,
our dog whistle voices above the ears of our assailants,

This is what survival sounds like.

The men speak to us like we are already dead.
Their eyes rove our curves like they are trying to decide,
how best to dispose of our bodies.

She Never Returned

She left her tent and never returned.
She exited the elevator and never returned.
She went out for coffee and never returned.
She locked her car and never returned.
She went to the office and never returned.
She got up from bed that morning and never returned.
She left her apartment and never returned.
She went to the gym and never returned.
And it was completely out of character.

She was so bright,
so funny,
so loved,
and she always showed up.

Except,
she left one day,
and never returned.

Alternate Heaven for Femicide Victims

When I tell you there should be a place
with a sign on the door that says "No Boys Allowed",
there is no asterisk.
No footnote for:
-nice boys
-little boys
-not boys at all.
And yes,
gender is a spectrum,
but this sign is not.
You know when you see it,
how we finger-painted it with our own blood,
how we marked our territory.
You can feel it in your gut.

No Boys Allowed !

And past the sign is a field,
a nightclub,
storefronts
of all the clothes we could dream of.
Here, your drink,
is just your drink,
and not a curse,
Here,
the scars are painted over in glitter,
we are our own universes.
A trail of stars from throat to navel.
Here,
your childhood is rainbows and unicorns.
Here,
your teen body is just a body.
Here,
we do not know the word femicide,
don't know what it is to have a man steal your breath.
Here,
we are our own heaven.

A Fear By any Other Name

I call my fear,
church.
The only place I go religiously.
I call my fear,
dust devil.
A thing that is only exciting to see from a distance.
I call my fear,
freeway rest stop.
The thing I never plan for but always end up at.
I call my fear,
mercury retrograde.
What I blame for all of my problems.

But most of all,
I do not have to call my fear,
it remembers my address,
it always sends a birthday card,
it is rarely late.
Is there even a word for something so certain?

The thing you can set your watch by.
The friend you'd be glad to see leave,
because at least you'd both be moving on.
Is there a word for waiting for a train,
and also wishing it never comes?

Is it just
awareness?
Is it vigilance?

Do you call it a ghost?
Do you call it a leech?
Do you call it to come over when you can't sleep?

The Men are Always Watching

While I pump my gas,
the man offers to check my tires.

While I browse the produce aisle for the ripest avocados,
the man says his grill makes the most tender steak.

While I am waiting for the cashier at the bookstore,
the man asks if I've ever read Bukowski.

While I am serving him at work,
the man asks if I have a boyfriend,
a husband,
if I'm one of those lesbians or something.

While I walk to my car,
the man shouts at me to show him my tits.

The men are always watching,
always hungry,
always waiting.

Habit

These instincts come as easy as breathing.
For example;
when the man with a window decal of a naked woman,
next to the bumper sticker boasting his short temper,
and ownership of a gun,
pulls his truck to the shoulder,
and lets me pass,
I check my rearview window every three seconds.

When he pulls back onto the road and follows me,
I pull in early to a parking lot,
wait for him to continue down the road,
check the mirrors again,
tap my fingers on the steering wheel,
turn off the music,
and listen to the stagnant air around me.
I take a deep breath before pulling out of the lot,
back onto the road.

I am late for work,
but at least I have arrived,
at least they don't call my phone five times,
before reaching my emergency contact.

I am walking in rushed and flustered,
but at least I am still walking,
at least I am still looking over my shoulder
instead of staring,
unblinking,
at whatever patch of desert sky,
I have been left under.

I am so tired of watching history be made
in the form of dead girls' bodies.

Things I Learned About Myself When Men Told Them to Me

1) I am only interested in true crime because serial killers like Bundy are "hot".

It cannot possibly be that I have been alive in this body long enough to see the lengths men will go to in order to peel me apart and spoon out the inside of me like a grapefruit. It cannot be that I have seen bodies like mine laid to rest, coffins empty or the missing posters that have been drenched in rain.

2) It is impossible for me to have an unbiased opinion of the newest case of 'Woman's Body Found' because I only blame men.

It is not because they found his fingerprints on her forearm, her thigh, the inside of her skirt. Not that they found his skin under her nails, his blood on her teeth, his hair clenched in her fist. When the man tells me with pride that he has never touched a woman without her consent, I know he is lying. That kind of smile is just bared teeth to the girl too afraid to speak. When he says "not all men" all I can hear is "take some responsibility, have some ownership over the fragility of our rage".

3) The reason I cannot stop listening to true crime podcasts is because I am fantasizing about being as famous as the dead girl.

It is not that I see myself in her obituary. The news put up a link to her social media and I looked up her Spotify playlists. The last song she listened to was the last song I listened to. What the man does not know is that it is a gift to remain ordinary. Waking up alone in my apartment is a rainstorm in June. I do not crave the fame of death but want the remarkability of being untouched.

4) I am one of those feminists who would see men be given curfews, I must want all of them locked away, I'm just another angry woman.

It cannot be that I used to teach children, and in my classroom no one was allowed to touch anyone else without permission. Gender be damned, every one of my students learned the word "consent". And maybe in this he is not wrong. Maybe when I tell him to teach his son not to rape instead of teaching his daughter ways to not be raped, what I am really saying is I do not trust you to raise tender men.

5) Secretly all women want to be dominated. I just want someone to control my every move

When the man pretends to choke me from across the room I hold my breath until I am blue and bulging around the eyes. I let my tongue swell and roll out of my mouth, I foam about the lips and collapse onto the ground. Isn't that what he meant when he said he wanted to own me? Isn't that what he said when he asked if my daddy knew where I was? Wasn't he asking for it?

The Men Are Always Talking

The man I share a cubicle with
tells the only other man in the office,
about his weekend.
About the girl he did coke with in the bar.
'I could have done whatever I wanted,
she was so far gone,
she wasn't even watching.
No one was there with her.'

And in this language,
the girl in the bar is:
Prey, and predator.
Bait and fish.
Hunted and hunter.
Because this man considers his presence,
an even exchange for her body.
And he set the trap,
offered her a bump,
bought her a drink,
but she took an Uber alone.
Didn't even give him her number.

And they call her gold digger,
call her tease,
call her a bitch.
But I have only known her
for the length of this conversation,
and I am just glad she made it home safe.

So Maybe My Room is a Mess

Once, I was told that detectives know
if the killer is a woman,
if the crime scene has been cleaned.

What they mean is,
men are most comfortable being seen,

when they can point to the bloody carpet and say,
he's been here.

Women always disappear,
women always make themselves smaller,

women always protect the witness,
from the trauma of the mess.

So maybe I leave my clothes on the floor,
leave my toothpaste on my mirror.

If I am missing,
I want the detectives to look at my apartment,

all of the half read books,
the coffee still warm in the pot.

I want them to look and say,
She's been here.

The Ways Fear Builds a Home in a Body

The man buying lingerie for his girlfriend
asks me to model the set,
and my shoulders tighten
under the weight of this expectation.
I feel the bite in my skin like a bra too tight.

The mechanic discounts my oil change
with his hand on the small of my back,
and the airbag of my lungs explodes into my ribs.
I cannot breathe around the burnt rubber smell of his skin.

The driver wants to know about my house,
who lives there with me,
did they leave me in this big house,
all alone?
My legs tense against the seat.
I am ready to leave this moving vehicle.
I ache for a long walk,
a bike ride on a hot June night,
to row a boat across the slick ocean surface.
Instead, I am running in a nightmare,
my body is tired but I've gained no ground.

I sleep in my sneakers.
I am always waking up gasping.
I am surprised by each new day.

Been Found Poem
(with excerpts found from twenty minutes of scrolling the crime section of a news site)

He's not even trying to call her phone,
he's not asking any questions,
any questions,
any questions,
any questions.

Considering there were six children in the house,
this could have been much worse.
He couldn't even lug groceries up the stairs.

This is just like a movie I watched on Netflix.
It's not unusual for the authorities to discover dead bodies,
dead bodies,
dead bodies,
dead bodies,
in the back of vehicles.

He hid her away and made it so no one could help her.
He plead not guilty,
not guilty,
not guilty,
not guilty.

He said he would drive her home.
Witnesses said they had a 'bad feeling'.
Witnesses said they reported a 'crazy guy' watching them.

She hasn't been found,
been found,
been found,
been found,
been found alive.

The Men are Always Helping

I work at a theater,
and one weekend a month I take the late shift.
It is two in the morning,
my back hurts from standing,
my cheeks hurt from my customer service smile.
My coworker offers to walk me to my car,
and in the empty parking garage,
as we circle the giant drain to my Camry,
he jokes that even if I screamed,
and the sound left my mouth,
bouncing off of every concrete pillar,
and eventually disappearing into the air,
No one would hear me.

Jokes that it was polite of me,
to bring my own car,
so he won't get blood in his trunk.

We stop at my car and the jokes stop with us.
He tells me to drive safe.
To buckle up.
To make sure my doors are locked.
Keep the neighborhood out,
you never know who will try to get in.

When they pulled her from the forest floor,
I swear we could still hear her scream.

When the trees that held her bones,
release their oxygen,
it sounds like a whimper,
like a blunt instrument,
like rope burn around the wrist.

Tangled

I don't know how to talk about grief,
without also talking about death.

What can I call the empty space inside of me?
Isn't it the place where he stuck the blade?
Isn't it the place where the bullet exited?
Isn't it the vein I emptied to feel full?

What else could I think when he stabbed her,
but that being in love can kill you?
What else can I do when he chokes me in bed,
but scratch until his skin is under my fingernails?
What else should I say when they ask me how I am,
but, *'at least I am alive'*?

I don't know how to grieve,
When there is a new dead woman
in the news each morning.
Do I call in sick to work?
Do I call my therapist?
Do I call an ambulance?

Maybe it is why I am always looking for signs,
why I pick up feathers from the sidewalk,
why I hear the ocean screaming along with me.
How can I bury the dead girl,
if I cannot grieve her?

How else can I tell you she smiled like I did,
in that photo of me wearing my favorite blue sweater?
How else can I tell you her favorite karaoke song
was my favorite karaoke song?
And how am I supposed to fall in love,
when I know the person meant to catch me
is cutting the ladder from the fire escape,
is taking the batteries out of my smoke detectors,
is pouring gasoline on my bedsheets?

Or maybe he isn't doing all of those things,
but he could.
I saw the gas can in his garage.
He took a packet of matches from the hotel we stayed in;
he asked me to kiss the label with my favorite red lipstick.

There is a word for giving someone the rope to hang you
and hoping they tether themselves to you instead.
A word for standing on a cliffs edge with his hands
on my shoulders.

Is it just love?
Is it only trust?
Is it writing my own obituary,
to save my mother the trouble of doing it?

The Unsub (Unknown Subject)
After the Characters and Stories of Criminal Minds

From the years of 2005-2020 crime show watchers around the world tuned in to watch a group in a fictional FBI Behavioral Analysis Unit solve grisly, ritualistic and serial murders across the nation. They referred to the killers they chased as "unsubs" or "unknown subject". For fifteen years a sometimes cyclical cast of characters became beloved parts of the viewer's lives. Not only were these characters fighting external evils, they faced their own demons at home. Because of this we can learn not all unsubs are the killers that lurk in the dark, but also some we see in the light.

Hailey tells Aaron to tender his resignation. She shouts at the bags under his eyes to leave his face, threatens his cracked lips and sore throat with eviction from his body. His shadow cowers further into the wallpaper and he swears she is taller today than she was yesterday. Reid can't beat the voice in his head at chess but insists his mother must take her medicine, even though it makes her groggy and she can't feel her teeth; she's sure they must be falling out.

> *And the unknown subject is everything*
> *we don't say to each other.*

Morgan is still running from the man with greedy hands but now he wears a bulletproof vest. He still can feel the calloused hands slide beneath the collars of his button downs, soon he's only wearing t-shirts.
The journalists press their stale vinegar breaths into JJ's hair as she details the wounds inflicted on the dead girl. They drool onto their notepads and press their open mouths to her cheeks. Thank her for the Pulitzers they are sure to win.

> *Here the unknown subject is the violence*
> *we inflict on each other every day.*

Emily notices a blue girl dripping wet out the corner of her eye. When she turns for a better look the girl's nose is pressed to her own,

freezing cold. Begging her to dredge the river, to find her body, she's sure it's there somewhere in the dingy gray of the shore.
While Spencer shoots up in the police station, his mother opens and closes her mouth inside the fishbowl of the institution. No one asks him about the track marks, or the bruises on his wrist the shape of a woman's hand.

> *And the unknown subject is the ghosts*
> *we keep just under our skin.*

Hailey's ghost is lingering in the floorboards and Aaron's flashlight ricochets off of her misty form. While his eyes dim, hers begin to shine. He watches her perch in dusty corners with old scrapbooks and a framed wedding photo, she scratches at the glass and Aaron's body bleeds.
Emily pulls a length of seaweed from her drain but the water still pools around her ankles in the shower. There is sand embedded in all her towels, the floormats of her car, in every corner of her desk at work.

> *This unknown subject is all of the skeletons*
> *we don't find buried in empty fields.*

Morgan runs into a burning building without a second thought, he's always had trouble breathing anyway. The pressure of the heat and the smoke is nothing compared to what he feels, finding the victim already gone, tied at ankles and wrists like a hog. And even though protocol insists he leave her as he found her, he sees his mother's laugh lines on the victim's face. He leaves the ropes behind to burn.
Garcia dreams of a party clown burying her body and wakes up screaming. She is strangling in her own sheets but cannot sleep until she finds the old purse she bought last summer, with its huge felt red pompom that always made her smile and then throws it down the trash chute of the apartment complex

> *The unknown subject is always dying*
> *or almost dying.*

JJ is always covered in the sweat of journalists who clamor around her, begging like baby birds for one more sickening detail. She cannot

wash the smell of ink from her skin and she stops buying newspapers altogether, deciding to only get her news from morning talk shows with perky hosts who drink vodka out of coffee mugs.
All of Emily's socks are wet, she squishes a hermit crab beneath her bare foot. The blue girl has brought a friend home, another dripping grey girl who begs her to bury the small crustacean surrounded by flowers. As she digs the girls insist, deeper, deeper.

> *Now, unknown subject is the dirt*
> *we can't scrub from our nails.*

Aaron grills a T-bone steak and watches hungrily as Hailey's ghost devours it, her teeth are filled with gristle and she doesn't stop until she's sucked the marrow from the bone. When she is satisfied with her after dinner bloat, she allows him to lick the mess off of her plate, he is just so happy to be full of anything.
Spencer gets in a fight with another passenger on the H train and no one has the heart to tell him he's arguing with an empty seat. When his coworkers ask why he is so angry he has no answer, no witty retort, no book to reference, it seems there are no words to describe the boiling of his own blood.

> *This unknown subject is the ways*
> *we starve ourselves to feed our demons.*

All of Garcia's pens break at once. Her desk is covered in glitter and feathers and sticky black ink. Her hands are smeared with their own small massacre. She wipes them on her pastel pink skirt and even when she does her laundry she cannot remove the stain.
Emily is woken up by a constant dripping and opens her eyes to three blue girls, soaked through and shivering. When they open their mouths to speak, all that comes out is a seagull's shrieking. When she begs them to tell her how to help them they inhale together, a tidal pull of force in her small apartment.

> *Here the unknown subject is the messes*
> *too deep to clean up.*

The killer takes his last breath in Reid's arms and although he shouldn't, he goes to the funeral. Watches the mother bury her child and for just a second, he can see himself inside the casket. He takes four days off work to visit his mother and resents her the entire time. Hailey waxes as Aaron wanes and Jack starts seeing his mother in reflections of every window he passes, he touches every glass he walks by and soon Aaron is only buying plastic.

> *Now, the unsub is not being able to look away*
> *from our own life's disasters.*

All of Emily's faucets pour out salt-water, lake-water, sewer-water, she always smells like the sea. The commuters on the A-train watch her with disgust, turn their noses away, hide their children from her, worried she is riddled with disease. They do not see the blue girls following her, do not hear the constant crashing of waves around their bloated bodies. Emily cannot get them to leave her alone. Morgan tells his sisters to call him while they walk through their parking garages at night. He listens to them breathe on the other side of the line, his heart clenching with every inhale as it waits for the exhale. They laugh and shake their heads at their overprotective brother but they do not know how many girls he's found that return home only half full.

> *And the unknown subject is the ways dead girls live*
> *and the ways alive girls die that no hero can prevent.*

The journalists have camped on JJ's lawn, rancid breath penetrating the doors and windows while they beg for more blood, for one more dead child, for one more headline. She fills the sprinkler system with bleach and rusted nails and turns it on full blast. Her lawn is dead but at least she is sleeping.
Garcia covers her ceilings in Christmas lights, she can't stand the dark anymore, she pays her electric bill in person, thanks each and every employee for helping her hide in the glow. Tells them about the monsters only she can find in the dark.

> *The unknown subject is the terrible things*
> *we do to rest easily in our beds.*

Aaron has begun sleeping on the floor, Hailey's ghost spreads out on their expensive mattress and he can smell her in his sheets, his towels, all of Jack's clothes. He is sure his lungs are fuller than a department store perfume aisle.

Morgan stays awake all night, breaking down walls in an empty house to build new ones in their place. When the sun rises and streams through the windows he can only see the shadows of the destruction he's left in his wake.

> *Here the unknown subject is the trail*
> *of evidence we each leave behind.*

The blue girls follow Emily in hoards, her clothes are always a little bit wet. When everyone orders in sushi she picks at her side of rice with disdain, everything tastes like salt. While she sits at the table, pours sugar in her coffee, the girls sit with her. When she looks up at them with tired eyes and begs them to tell her where they are, they step forward one by one. The river, the lake, the well in rural Ohio, in the middle of the ocean. There are so many places to hide a dry body, Emily has to make a list.

Reid is certain the reflection in the mirror is winking at him. He is sure the whispers he hears in the library are his own voice. He is positive his head is cracking open. He hates the doctor's office, resents the pills and intake forms, but every time the doctor assures him it's only stress, just lack of sleep, just anxiety from the job, he breathes a little easier. Calls his mother and assures her he is her kin, he doesn't even resent the nurse for telling him she's gotten worse. The air is lighter in D.C tonight, when he gets to keep his mind a little bit longer.

> *This unknown subject is the small victories*
> *we trudge through life to get by.*

Jack keeps asking Aaron where his daddy is. He doesn't recognize the skeleton tucking him in at night. All he sees is Hailey, she is taking up all of the space, she is eating all of their food, taking all of the toys from the cereal box. Finally, Aaron's had enough, he walks into the crystal shop on Third Street and buys four bundles of sage, lights one in every corner of the house, waits for the smoke alarms to go off and then lights them again. He hires a psychic to come and force the spirit away. Finally, when the house is quiet and Jack is sleeping soundly. He grills a steak, eats the whole thing in front of the mirror and smiles a bloody smile while he licks the plate clean.

JJ passes her last test, gets a perfect score on the fire-arms exam, now when the journalists clamor to her like desperate baby birds seeking their mother, she nudges them aside with her shoulder. Flips her hair and stomps away, she only smells like vanilla now, she never reads the paper, she saves the girls before they are headlines. When she is home she lets her boys run around on their dead lawn, nothing will ever grow there but she's begun to love the color brown anyway.

> *Now, the unknown subject is the ways*
> *we nourish ourselves by starving our enemies.*

Morgan goes to the funeral of the man whose hands he knows better than his own. His mother insists he stays home, his sisters beg him to go to the movies instead. He wears a yellow suit, a ray of sunshine breaking apart the black cloud of grief. When he passes the boys playing basketball in the neighborhood they stop and cheer, they cry tears of relief, he makes a shot from the three-point line and whistles the whole way home.

Garcia buys new pens, she likes the ink with glitter on the inside, she goes to the carnival and takes pictures of herself with all of the clowns, she frames them and covers the walls of her office with them. When she fills out her casework, detailing the evidence she found on the murderer's computer, she uses a neon orange highlighter. She signs her name in glitter glue. She puts scratch and sniff stickers on every page. When the director begs her to stop, and when they think she can't find any more room for color, she prints it on rainbow construction paper, and now everyone else is covered in her, they can't ever escape her even after she's gone.

> *At last, the unknown subject is daring to stay alive*
> *despite all of the things trying to kill you.*

What is the word for the place
where a dog is put down
for being an animal
and men who are monsters
get to be kings?

I call it America,
America,
America.

An Interlude for My Mother, Who Wishes I'd Watch More Comedies.

I don't always present my grief as clean and round,
as a freshly polished stone.
I've been talking so much of my fear,
now let me tell you the things I love.

I love Chloe's gold jewelry.
I love watching a dog with its head out a car window.
I love the shriek of children at a waterpark.
I love cold coffee and hot tea.
I love my sister's cooking.
I love painting my fingernails black and my toenails pink.
I love scratching things out with a pen.
I love making a mess when I'm baking cookies.
I love my niece's soft yellow hair.
I love hearing my grandmother order breakfast.
I love knowing the names of constellations.
I love when kids make up their own jokes.
I love when teenagers go trick or treating.
I love when my uncle sings along to Dean Martin songs.
I love the first step into a pool on the hottest day in spring.
I love finding a pen in my purse right when I need one.
I love when my parents have an entire conversation in movie quotes.
I love taking naps with a dog.
I love sucking on ice cubes in December.
I love England in the fall, and Norway in the spring.

Thank you mom,
I think I needed that.

Things I Know from Spending Most of My Life Around Women

Cold water is best to get blood out of anything,
we are always cleaning up crime scenes.

Once when a boy broke my heart,
he offered to stay and hold me while I cried,
but I have been cleaning my own blood
out of the sheets for years now,
surely I can hold my own heart in my hands.

It is always best to laugh at the joke first,
if you don't,
everyone looks to you for permission.
Also you can laugh through almost anything,
if you fake it long enough,
and we are so used to faking it.

If you can't say it in words,
use a song,
borrow the melody from another throat,
they like it when you speak silent anyway.

Bubblegum on the carpet will come up easily,
if you let an ice cube melt on top of it first,
if it is in your hair,
try peanut butter.
If it's nail polish on the floor,
just buy a new rug,
we know all of the best ways
to cover up our own hot pink messes.

If you are stung by a jellyfish at the beach,
and are surrounded by only female bodies,
you can use Windex to dull the pain.
Someone is sure to have some in their car,
at the house,
at the bottom of their purse.

We are creatures of habit,
who have been told we never see things clearly,
we are used to taking the smudge out of the equation
before we start the problem.

If you are in a car and feel unsafe,
pull your hair out at the root and leave it,
everywhere.
Touch every surface,
leave yourself bald,
if it means someone will catch your killer.

A man will never ask you for help,
even if they need it.
So when he walks up to you in the grocery store parking lot;
say no,
scream,
run,
fight first.
It is better to ask forgiveness,
than to never ask for anything again.

Keep an up to date picture ready on your computer,
just in case you go missing.
Ask your mother for one,
she'll pick one that you hate,
but it will be the one that looks most like you.
Let her hold it up to the cameras,
let them see her cry,
so somewhere another girl will call her mother,
and ask her to pick out a picture,
just in case.

The Grief and the Promises

The living are forgetful;
only the dead remember,
and they hold grudges.

Patroclus is dead and cannot rest,
don't they know he is lost without his Achilles?
Didn't they hear how he called him his most beloved,
his heart outside his chest?
Achilles slept with a ghost,
would take no food or wine,
why should he be full when his lover never would be?

Even the Gods could hear his cries.
the ocean floor shook with his grief,
when he called out,
'Patroclus'.
When he called out,
'Home'.

Odysseus is haunted,
he wakes in the night,
sticky with sweat,
but shivering,
the mouths of the young warriors open,
swarms of locusts tumble from their throats.
a dreadful hum of broken promises.

They haunt him there in the battlefields of Troy,
which still reek of blood and the cries of dying men.
They haunt him on the sea,
with each day his journey is lengthened,
he can feel the lover's hands pressing into him.
They haunt him in Ithaca,
asleep with his queen,
the boys stand at the foot of the bed,
and stare with their eye sockets empty,
and unblinking.

But their hands are still young,
They still hold each other like they are their own anchors.
And finally, it is written in stone,
their ashes entangled as limbs in their bed.
Finally, the living are no longer haunted,
and the dead hold no more grudges,
but only memory.

First Timer

I believe in past lives,
but my mother says this must be my first time,
must be my first of everything.
I want to hate her for saying it,
I want to be angry at her perceived innocence of me.
I am never surprised,
and also always surprised.

I think,
in her way,
it is a way of reminding me,
that all of my feelings are new.

I am always feeling things in capital letters,
I am always in love or heartbroken.

I think,
in her way,
it is a way of telling herself I am getting all of the bad,
out of the way now,
so that next time,
I will have learned my lessons.

When the first boy told me he would not love me,
I sobbed broken into the phone,
I asked her why,
why, why
what is wrong with me?
And maybe she knows,
that the first break hurts the most.
So this must be the first time my soul,
has ever cried broken.

I tell her I am afraid,
of how much I love my nieces:
how I would slit my own wrists
if they needed my blood;

how I would walk into the desert,
if it meant they would always have clean water to drink.

I tell her I will never have children,
because I am afraid of the way,
I love things too much.
My favorite pair of sneakers
with holes in the toes,
ripped fabric at the heels.
How I hate watching finale episodes
of my favorite shows.

Maybe she's right,
this must be my first time,
every sunset must be brand new,
every word must be waiting to be written.

Maybe she is just teaching me
how to say goodbye.

All the Bars are Funeral Homes

There is a bar in my town,
that used to be a funeral home,
like an actual funeral home.
The benches are old pews,
all of the lanterns are gothic.

It's made me think about all the bars,
and all the funeral homes,
and all of the things they have in common.

Like mourning,
the people who sit inside of them,
mourning something,
or someone,
or both.

And consuming,
how we are all trying to fill ourselves,
with something to make us more alive.

And also people,
who find themselves,
only coming together at these places,
how all of the stories they have of each other,
sprout from here.

And also maybe celebrating life,
and love,
and daring your body to keep breathing,
even here.
In this place where everything
is begging you to poison yourself.

For Wanda and the Hex

They named you a witch,
bestowed it upon you,
like a badge of honor.
Told you to wear it with pride,
but answer for your sins,
the sins of your brother,
of your captain.

They forced this power upon you,
but did not show you how to use it,
or where to replace the battery,
or what it would be like
to feel more than your body can hold.
They will blame it on your sex:
this recklessness,
such a sad woman,
that poor girl.

But I know better,
I watched my father,
grieve his father,
watched the incinerator of his mouth,
open and shut for a pill,
that would help him dream a world
where they were together.

They will blame it on circumstance:
that poor dear,
her poor lost love.
Like a body does not still hold
a part of who it once was:
like his smile is no longer his smile,
his hands no longer his hands.

But I saw my grandmother cry
at the sight of her husband's ashes.
Watched her pack up all of his clothes,

she knew a body was still a body,
even with nothing inside of it.
And his body was not there
to wear his favorite shirts;
his body was not in the urn
but in the furnace.
The kiln of her heartbreak.
And you, too, know
what it is to want to hold a body,
in both hands.

They will never call you merciful,
never label what you are doing,
for what it is:
your best.

When you crave home,
when the ache in your ribs
starts to feel like
your mother's perfume,
your father's favorite teacup,
you lasso it into your lap.

When your boys look at you,
hungry for a map to themselves,
you bring them a buffet,
call it "brother".

And I watched my mother,
grieve her sister.
If she could bring her back today,
I know that she would,
because if I could bring her back today,
I would,
and don't we always grow into our mothers?

Watch them spit out your home,
pry it from between their molars,
and flick it at you from across the table.

They name it Hex,
a spell fit for a witch,
or perhaps,
a wake
fit for her love,
a life
fit for her children.

Perhaps just a day:
one,
single,
day,
where no one cries.

Elegy

The sad girl at the counter says,
a boy she knew once is dead
and she doesn't know how to feel.
I shatter the icy lake between us with an anecdote.
I say,
do you want to hear something weird?
The first guy I hooked up with,
killed himself a year later,
I don't think the two are related,
but I guess you never know.
I shrug and now the girl is laughing.

She says hers was serving,
5 to 10 for aggravated robbery,
says the gun he used
was kept under the pillow when she slept there.
And now the frost between us is a summer breeze,
now we are both girls collecting dead boys,
and this is how we have something in common.
She asks my boys name,
but the truth is I don't know.
I tell her the name is not part of the story,
I didn't keep it like a trophy.
I didn't know him like that.
I tell her to forget his name,
her dead boy,
say it one last time,
taste it on your tongue,
memorize the texture,
how your lips curl around it,
and then never say it again.
Let him rest,
I say,
let him be,
keep only the memory,
but do not hold him hostage.

I Grieve the Girl I Would Have Been

I think if my mother were not my mother,
I would be the kind of person who needs,
every decision to be made for them.
I think I'd be a drinker.
I think I'd know how to change a tire,
but always have someone around to do it for me.
I think I would not be afraid of birds.
I think I would never say no and mean it.
I think I would have shitty taste in television.

I think if my father were not my father,
I would have learned too late,
to be cautious of men.
I think I would not have to watch the door,
from my booth at the diner.
I think I would not be disgusted at the thought,
of pulling my own hair from the drain.

I think if my parents were not my parents,
I would have said "I love you" to more people,
and not meant it.
I think I wouldn't know,
how to hold a small and fragile thing properly,
to cradle the head,
stroke the cheek,
coo softly.

I think if we were not each other's,
I would not know how to do things softly.
I want to be both of us and neither all at once.
I wonder if somewhere,
on some distant shore,
the girl I would have been is thinking the same thing.

Things I Should Have Said at the Funeral and After

I never had an imaginary friend,
I couldn't commit to the fantasy.
If you were my imaginary friend I think
I wouldn't have committed to you either.
I am so afraid of committing to anything.
I have so many habits and none of them are good.

Did you ever see the sun rise over the ocean?
It looks like the world is laying out its long silver tongue.
The water looks like mercury.
I love the way oil looks in a parking lot after it has rained.
I think the prettiest things are poisonous
but I can't stop putting them inside of me.
My favorite color green never grows here.
If your favorite color was my favorite color would you move
somewhere it grew?
Would you want it outside all of your windows?
Would you rub yourself in poison ivy just to be close to it?
I think I would.

Sometimes I get the urge to hurt myself
and I have to do something to stop it.
I have to chew off all my fingernails,
I have to eat all of the ice cubes in the freezer.
I have to put something in my mouth that can't kill me until the
feeling passes.

Do you know how long an hour feels
when there's nothing good on tv?
Of course you don't, you always knew how
to find something good on tv.

Did they tell you, wherever it is you went,
they killed off your favorite character in the show we watched?
Did they tell you I cried and felt like you'd died all over again?

I can't stop picking at the skin around my nails.
Do you have a remedy for that?
Can you fix all of my bad habits?

Let's go shopping.
When I get angry at the dressing room mirror
we can split a Cinnabon.
We can get makeovers at the Chanel counter.
You can buy me new sheets.
I haven't slept since you died.
I don't know how to anymore.
I can't find anything you hand wrote.
I want to be the kind of friend
that is easy to get a hold of
but typing on my phone takes too long.

I found the perfect kind of pen,
it glides just the way I like over paper.
Did you have a favorite pen?
Do you think it's with your things?
Where are all of your things?
I have your bracelet in my car,
I hide it because I'm afraid of it breaking.
It's not that I'm hiding from you,
I just know that I'm breaking.
I am almost always breaking or broken.

Did you ever break a bone?
Have you ever felt itchy under a cast?
That is how I feel all of the time.
An itch I can't reach even with a pencil.
I don't know where to visit you.
Where do I mail you a Christmas card
if you don't have a grave?

Don't change your schedule for anyone.
Don't care about people who don't care about you.
I learned that the hard way.
You never cared about what people said, did you?
Of course you didn't.

I am always learning things too late.
I am always finding your footsteps in my path.
I am always sending you pictures
of things you've already seen.

Why am I so willing to die for everything?
But afraid of believing in anything?
Don't smile for longer than you have to,
eventually it just looks like you're baring your teeth.
Don't bare your teeth.
Don't let them know the strength of your jaw
until it's wrapped around their wrist.
Did anyone ever tell you
not to bite the hand that feeds you?
They must have.
I am always foaming at the mouth,
always screaming with my jaw unhinged.

Do you remember I was born a day late?
Maybe it's not the kind of fact people recall.
I think about it all the time.
I have been running late ever since.

I know I've been talking about myself too much.
I don't know how to talk about you
without feeling like I'm cursing.
Without feeling like I'm saying Bloody Mary
into the bathroom mirror.
Like all of the air has been sucked out of the room.

Resting is for the dead, grief is for the living.
I was never good at saying goodbye.
I don't like watching the final episodes of tv shows.
I hate endings,
I hate speaking my feelings
but love going to therapy.
I think I just like being able to speak
for forty five full minutes
without anyone interrupting me.

Were you ever so good at something
that you felt it in your blood?
That it consumed your every thought?

Really think about it,
let it sit underneath your skin,
pry the answer out with your teeth,
tear at it like a hangnail
until your answer is a bleeding wound.
Tell me when you find it.
I'll help you clean the blood.
I'll help you find a band-aid.
I'll tell you my answer too.

Maybe it'll be one more thing
we have in common.

I love seeing balloons float into the sky,
but I never release them,
on account of the ocean,
because they fill the fragile throats
of sea creatures.

And you can never miss the dead
as much as you can love the living.

The Sun Mourns Icarus

They called you crazy,
silly, bird brained boy.
They begged for response,
from your cherry lips.
They eagerly awaited an opportunity,
to look down onto you instead of up.
From where they stooped,
the air is filthy on the low road.

They just weren't as inventive as you.
Didn't see the genius behind your fiery amber eyes.
The eyes that looked at me and saw adventure.
You saw me as a friend instead of an enemy,
you sang my name instead of cursing my existence.
Instead of praying for rain you danced in my drought.
I only wanted to hold your hand,
only wanted to caress your cheek,
only wanted to run my fingers through your curls
and kiss your eyelids closed.

I could have watched you forever,
when you took to the air,
when you whooped and squawked
your excitement into the clouds.
You twisted and turned on the breeze,
showing even the birds that they had been,
missing out on something all this time.
I shone brightest for you that day,
knew how you liked it
when I made the ocean like jewels,
when you turned to me,
open mouthed and laughed
your siren laugh,
I longed to laugh with you,
so much it burned.
I wanted to watch you so closely,
I couldn't bring myself to blink.

I had to watch the whole bloody mess.
Each drip worse than the last,
the sizzle a harmony of dread.

I called out to you,
knowing you could not hear me,
that I could not run to catch you.
And soon you were falling,
plummeting to the ground
like a summer storm you always loved,
like a lightning strike.

Your body was a cannonball,
you left a streak in the sky like gunpowder.
In the end, they blamed me.
My vicious heat, my savage tongue,
licking at your wings,
each evening I set they rejoiced,
only to cry out in the mornings.
Calling out your name:
Icarus.
Icarus.
Icarus.
If only they knew,
I still have not blinked.
I'll love you until my last light is gone.
My sweet,
soaring,
songbird.

The Gum Tree

There is a plaque on a wall,
for every student of my high school,
who died before graduation.
And in front of the death wall,
a gum tree.
Minty Trident,
sweet Juicy Fruit,
spicy Big Red,
globs of hot pink Hubba Bubba.
We don't know when it started,
Or when the janitors stopped bothering,
to scrape the pieces off.

All we knew is the need,
to pull something from inside of us,
To yank a sample of ourselves,
that is loud and gnashing,
to put something hot and alive,
and stick it to this place
where everything is dirt and rust and stone.

A secret only we know:
sometimes feeling something in your bones
is stronger than knowing it in your brain.

When The Marvel Women Have Dinner

Despite all the distance,
and time,
and kittens stuck in trees,
and fires needing drenched,
and men breathing in all the fresh air,
once a year,
the women of Marvel get together.
A sort of Congress or conference, or club.

They order favorite dishes,
bring tastes of home to share.
And as they share plates,
and stories, and breaths.

They laugh,
at all of the silliness of the past,
the inconsistency of the present,
the uncertainty of the future.
They sit in silence,
for one minute,
for each one of them lost.
Some years it feels like eons,
others it feels like only seconds,
but at the end,
they raise their glasses and say together:
We have lived, we have lost,
but most of all; we have loved.
And always too soon,
it is time to leave each other again,
but as they embrace in goodbyes,
they breathe in the space between each other.

Sisterhood, which is to say, savage love,
the thing that sets their pulses
in time with each other.

An October Afternoon

After they'd laid a flag,
over her shrunken body.
After they'd cleared,
the last of her away.
The rooms were still not empty.
She was everywhere,
her photos,
her music,
her favorite coffee mugs.

Her smell still hung in the air,
and we walked around the space of her.
Like she was still sitting there.
Like they both were.

Perhaps inside all of us is a gallery
of the people we love,
and the tears we will cry for them.

We are all wondering
when this dam will crumble and empty,
when this gallery will hold only memories
and not the violent sound
of our collective hearts breaking.

The Moon and the Sea

The fat, full moon hangs yellow on the horizon.
It takes up the whole of the sky
and casts a lantern glow on the ocean below it.
The light is kissing the water but cannot keep it warm,
and the sea can stretch its limbs into the air,
weighed down and heavy with salt and gravity,
but it can never touch the shore of this distant lover.
Instead, it rages with a violent crash,
turning stone to sand.

While the children shriek and play in the tide,
the sea is wailing, longing for the moon.
The moon is thinning, waning with sorrow,
in the inky black distance from its love.
How badly it wants to swim,
in the valley of its deepest trench,
to hunt for treasure among its ruins,
to know where it hides,
whatever it hides from human hands.

The moon is a sliver of light in the distance,
hard to see it among the lights of ships and cruise-liners,
where grubby faces press into the glass,
and fill the air with the stink of the living and the loud.
In the distance the whales are singing,
they are following the ebb and flow of the waves,
and call to the moon: Please don't go away.
Where do you go when you leave?
Who else do you pull on if it is not the sea?
The moon is too far away to be heard,
but it is crying out as well:
There is no other,
I go nowhere,
but instead am pushed from you,
by the cruelty of the Earth's relentless spin.
There is,
no one,

no one,
no one,
but you.

Living Deadly

If these sins are what ends me, I'm already dead.

I have felt anger so strong,
it makes my bones shake inside me,
each step a quake crumbling the streets to dust.
A rage that plummets the body straight to hell,
it buzzes in the ears like angry hornets.

And I have died the sweetest death in sleep,
every Sunday morning,
wrapped in fresh sheets and lover's arms.
I have spent days on the beach,
rising for nothing but the sea.

When I grab at my lover with both hands,
what I mean is,
if I would die today, I'll do it from inside of you,
if your lips are my poison,
I am still eager for your kiss.

I have looked out at the ocean,
wanting to swallow it whole,
seen a deep green forest,
and thought of burying myself in it.

I am the black hole,
and the space it feeds on.
I want to be all of it,
everything, all at once.

If I am destined to die by this,
I am lucky to be my tomb,
so pleased to write my own epitaph.

I will hold my own hand,
stroke my own hair,
kiss my own lips.

I am glad to fill myself now,
to make all of the days I was empty, ache.

All of the time I punished this heavy body,
let the graveyard stretch open for me.

And if I will be killed,
let my jealousy pull the trigger,

let the manhole cover boiling,
at the edge of my chest tie the noose.

If these sins are fated to be my end,
no one call the funeral home,
no one choose a casket.

I am already gone.

Men Who Have Held Me

When I am afraid,
I dream about the men who have held me,
even if only in my mind.

The boy I had a crush on in high school,
before I knew what you believe in is important.
I dream his face is telling me he loves me,
I dream he kisses my hair,
I dream I tell him all my secrets and they disgust him,
they make him take his hands off of me like they burn him.

When I wake up I think it must have been real,
I touch my cheeks,
still warm from the pillow,
and the palms of my hands blistering from the heat.

I dream about the first boy I loved,
how he preferred to touch someone else's skin,
how he kissed me like a chore.

In my dream he begs me to take him back,
kneels before me and promises to hold me,
with both hands this time.
At first I turn up my nose at him.
I toss my hair over my shoulder.
I am his saviour.
I am his saint.

When I say he has one more chance,
that is when a friend finds me,
whispers to me that he prayed at another girl's altar,
saw him take her communion, her body and blood.

And when I wake up I think I can smell her perfume,
I can hear their lips touching.
It makes me take a shower and scrub my skin raw.

I dream of the man I wish would hold me.
The one who does not know what I look like
without makeup,
or naked,
Who still thinks my teeth have never felt,
the crash of a curse word rolling off of the tongue.
I think of all the new ways this man will hurt me,
how we will hurt each other.

When I wake up I can still feel the safety of his arms,
and when the sun comes through my blinds
the feeling of him fades.

My ribcage is empty,
the lion of my lungs is gone,
has escaped and is now prowling down the road
looking for something new
to sink her teeth into.

Don't You Have a Bed Partner?

After the first of everything,
you asked me if you should stay.

Something about early classes,
and needing a shower.

So I lied when I said you should go get some rest,
that I slept better on my own anyway.

Left you with a kiss in the cold English air,
that swept under the front door.

I held the collar of your jacket and zipped it up to your chin,
I didn't want you to catch a cold on your walk home.

I crawled into my bed,
didn't change the sheets,
my pillows smelled like your scalp.
I cried, but in a good way.

The next morning, when my roommates asked
where you were, with a wink and quirked brow,
I told them the truth.
I was afraid of my snoring.
that my uncontrolled heavy breath,
would push you away.
Force our fairytale into reality.

I wanted you to love me so much,
I would lie awake all night,
risk collapsing in the hallway,
for you to look at me,
the way you never had,
the way you never would.

I only know how to build homes inside of people,
but don't actually know how to live inside of them.
I am so obsessed
with being someone's all-consuming love
but I can't stand to look at myself
in the mirror for too long.

The first girl I loved,

was a new student,
with pink streaks in her hair,
pristine manicured nails.
She smoked cigarettes she stole,
from the seniors outside the school.
Her tank top was always perfectly disheveled,
the smallest sliver of pale hipbone,
on display to the sun.
Her skin seemed to glow in it,
her bleached hair rivaled Marilyn Monroe's,
the bored way she took notes in class,
reminiscent of a Rhodes scholar.

Her brother was also beautiful,
gold to her silver,
sharp edges to her soft lines,
Apollo and Artemis gracing our small suburb,
making everything technicolor,
making our collective breaths catch in our throats.
We were in awe of them.
He never spoke much but was always mid conversation,
always the main attraction,
but I bought the ticket for her sideshow.
How she hovered around the edges,
but laughed the loudest.
The bravest thing I ever did,
was call her name across a room.

My most daring declaration,
was to shout out of the closet,
to crack open the door,
to let in a sliver of her sun,
and bathe in it,
for as long as she allowed it.

Moonsong

When Romeo stared up to the window,
and asks Juliet to rise,
to kill the envious moon,
sick and pale,
I wanted Juliet to pull the sash.
Close the blinds,
Snuff the candles.

An early night to bed for his fair sun.
I wonder if they knew
the moon was the only one
keeping their secret,
her pale face witnessing their first of everything.

I wonder if the moon watched on,
smirking, head shaking. and thinking,
Earth's children never seem to learn,
and first love to them feels like inventing the wheel.

And what would Shakespeare say?
Would he say:
we cannot write poems without her
when there is no first kiss?
Without the touch of her light?
When I cannot talk about you,
without her glow?

The Ways I've Loved You

If all of your freckles are kisses from past lives,
then I have loved your shoulders most.
In every life I have placed my lips
on the warm curve of your jaw.
The point where your hair sprouts from your temple
must have been my haven.
I must have praised your hands, each lumpy knuckle.
I must have kissed your ring fingers and promised you forever.
If you had fallen down I would have kissed your knees,
knobby and knocking and restless to dance.

If each freckle is a place I have kissed,
then I must have worshipped your nose,
it's perfect placement on the plane of your face.
I must have needed to taste the sun,
on the highest points of you, I must have savored it,
the golden scattering across your cheeks.
If my lips were the paintbrush and you were the canvas,
I would have created a masterpiece,
and would hang it in The Louvre,
and label it in gold embossed letters: "The Lovers".
My signature on every corner of you.

If each of your freckles are kisses from past lives,
then I have loved you well in each of them.

And when I find uncharted waters on the map of your skin,
when a new pale valley lays out before me
unfurled from the country of you,
I will chart new constellations;
new mythologies for future generations to look upon,
thrill to, point to and say;

>*There,*
>*there is where love once lived.*
>*It left its mark,*
>*for all of time.*

Girls Like Me Don't Know How to be Quiet

The boys in the bar hush me for talking too loud
and shout at the game on tv.
The girls in line for the concert,
snicker while I take a picture of my best friend,
in the golden hour sun.
The elderly couple at the coffee shop,
glare as I type furiously on my keyboard.

It's just that girls like me
have too many wishes wasted on stars,
and quarters tossed into fountains,
and birthday candles.

It's just that girls like me
are always stomping too hard,
clapping in the silence,
cheering when we should be whispering.

Girls like me have too much Athena,
Artemis,
Aphrodite.
Too much,
I know I'm smart,
I know I'm tough,
I know you love me.

When my mother looks frantically over her shoulder,
when my sisters roll their eyes,
when my cousins call me "wild one".
I want to kiss their foreheads,
braid their hair away from their face,
look them in the eye and ask them,
"Who do you think taught me
how to be a
        girl
        like
        this?".

Summer

It was the summer between training bras and padded cups,
when our big sisters put playboy bunny stickers
on their hip bones to make sun-tanned tattoos.
And we ate fruit instead of popsicles to stay skinny,
shameful of our pudgy girl bodies.
And we rode our bikes in the golden hour,
and only pretended they were our mighty steeds
when we were alone.

It was the summer of our first boy-girl parties when it mattered.
When everyone skipped my birthday to share a warm beer
with twelve people in the basement down the street.
And I still didn't have boobs and the bikini top
betrayed the hideous secret I spent all of seventh grade keeping.

It was the summer before college,
when it all passed in a sweaty haze,
and we were sticky with cheap vodka.
And I stayed up for three days binge drinking
and doing one thousand jumping jacks because
the internet said it would burn one whole pound.
I hated everything, including myself except for the times
when I looked up from the bottom of a bottle.

It was the summer between early and mid-twenties,
when we were a patchwork of SPF.
100 on our faces, 15 on pale white bullies
50 on our always exposed limbs,
and we only swam to cool off and not to play.
But we shared books and lip gloss,
and sang karaoke until 3 in the morning.
And we told each other we loved us
for learning how to love us,
And it was hot and we were sweaty,
but we were home,
and realized we always had been.

If I were a God,

perhaps I would be Dionysus,
I would drink wine and let people love me without feeling guilty.

Or maybe, I would be Athena,
I would sit and sketch and philosophize until night turned today.

Perhaps I would be Nyx,
flick my eyeliner and dye my hair and throw my own mosh pit.

Or I'd like to be Zeus,
to see what it is like to live as a man with no consequences,
to strike each lover to the ground with lightning.

I would maybe be Hermes, god of messaging,
what would it be like to never be left unread? I wonder.

I could be Aphrodite, with her pink blushed cheeks
and perfectly mussed hair. I would love everyone including myself.

I should like to be Apollo, if only so every poem I write would rhyme.

I wonder, could I be Hades and Persephone,
goddess of spring flowers and hellfire.

I could be Ares, letting all of my rage fall under the umbrella of war.
To yell and be heard.

I would like to be Hecate, to be prayed to and invoked
whenever I am most needed.
If I were a god, I would like to be loved, but not revered,
to be held, but not a captive,
to be a savage with manners.

Show me a god like that,
and perhaps then,
I will kneel and pray.

I Don't Remember My Teen Years

I just feel like they happened to a smaller version of me.
Smaller in distance, though also in size,
I just remember feeling like every day
was the precipice of something.
Like if I didn't curl my eyelashes everyone would notice,
everyone would see.
I just remember introducing myself a lot to kids I'd known forever,
who's living rooms we'd lie in side by side
tucked into sleeping bags, whose tents were next to mine
on camping trips.

I was preparing for an interview every time I spoke.
I remember thinking if I couldn't pass my math test,
I wouldn't be allowed back home,
I would sleep outside with the dog
even though our dog slept inside.
I remember thinking what a waste it was,
to spend so much time at a place,
that could not spell my name.
I remember recruitment day.
The men in pressed uniforms
who swore the barracks were safe for women
but never had a woman there to verify it.
I remember sitting in the empty bathtub
with my music turned up
while my sister and parents fought
like waiting for a tornado.

I was always preparing for a disaster.
I remember feeling too big for my skin.
I was always feeling something,
and so much of it.

Maybe it was the undiagnosed personality disorder,
or the fact that people spoke through me instead of to my face.
But I remember thinking if I wasn't there no one would notice.

I used to dare myself to go a whole day without speaking
but there was always a theater rehearsal,
always a question to be answered,
always a joke to laugh at.

I remember laughing a lot.
I remember making people laugh.
Maybe I can't remember my teen years
because I carry her with me.
The small but distant girl,
her fear of her own shadow,
her willingness to try anything once,
her need to only cry in private.

Sometimes I see her in the mirror,
sometimes I hold her hand,
sometimes I tell her I love her,
sometimes she says it back

New Vocabulary

The first time I saw the word *"melancholy"*,
was in a book that I'd known first as a movie.
A kind of sadness that makes you want more of it,
A brand of hurting in the heart like a bruise on the skin;
you press your fingertips into it
to make sure that it still has its own pulse.

In the book a woman hung empty liquor bottles,
on a tree out front, the windchimes of her addiction.
At my age I did not understand that addiction,
is a way of saying 'the thing I would have let kill me'.

The adults told me, I had an addictive personality
I thought it meant:
'I never want you to change',
'you make everything better by being yourself',
'we are addicted to the way you make us laugh like children'.

What I did not hear is my mother's girlhood cries
every time her father left again.
I did not hear the betrayal of my grandmother,
once again, recognizing the perfume on her husband's collar.
So when I was very young,
wanting to flaunt my new vocabulary,
I told the teacher I was feeling melancholy
but could not answer why.
It seemed like a simple explanation
for the way I knew I would die someday.
The thought that haunted me,
when I was away from home,
was anything might happen while I was gone
and I would not be there to stop it.

When I told my friend I had an addictive personality
she wanted to know my vice.
What did I love more than myself?
What did I fall asleep clutching on the couch?

What ways would I mirror the people who hurt her?
But I couldn't explain that I just loved jumping into the pool,
from the tallest diving board.
That I would walk in and out of the water,
up and down the ladder,
hold my stomach in my throat for the seconds-long drop,
if it meant for those moments
I was not of this earth.

I didn't know how to tell her,
that I love the sound of other people's laughter,
that when I went without it too long,
I felt desperate to say something funny.

When I first heard the word *'cult'*.
I heard *'community'*.
I heard *'the place the world cannot touch you'*.
And by then I did not need to flaunt my new language.
I did not need the crash and burn of feeling a word,
so deep in my bones,
even when I do not know what it means.

Instead, I knew I was in danger.
I knew I was easy prey,
knew I would need to look
over my shoulder just in case.

This was a bruise I could not dig into,
this was a hurt I could not check on,
but I would always know it was there.

Persephone

When I put my hands in the cool water
and pinch and pull the flesh of the ripe pomegranate,
I am thinking of the washerwomen.
Washerwomen who would gather in groups of dozens on laundry day,
who would wring their husbands' sweat and stink from their sheets,
and talk about the news of the village,
of the girl who was caught with a boy after curfew;
how they too were once girls risking getting caught with a boy
just for the pleasure of dancing in the sticky hot night
and being held like something that would shatter.

When my freshly manicured nails push,
into the sponge of the pomegranate and I swipe my fingers
gently across the inside to loosen the seeds from its grip,
I am thinking of community:
of how I wish I had a group of women to chat with
about the news of the day right now;
of how I wish I had a group of women to help me
hang my wet clothes;
how I wish to have a group of women to hold
my head for me when my neck is too tired.
I am so tired. I feel like I haven't slept in days.

While I listen to the crack of the pomegranate skin,
as I pull its seeds from it, I am thinking of Persephone.
How she was free to go to Hades,
so long as she did not eat or drink.
You can only be happy if you are empty.
I wonder if Hades kneeled before her,
hot molten tears in his eyes as he begged her,
please, please for me, don't waste away like this.
I wonder if he kissed every inch of her,
and worshipped her fullness,
her hips, her breasts, her arms.
If he held her and promised,
"You can leave but please don't disappear.
I don't know how to make it without you."

I peel the pomegranate underwater,
to keep my hands from being stained,
and I think of the six seeds under Persephone's tongue;
how they must have teased her with the promise of sweetness.
I wonder if, when she feels them in her mouth,
she thinks of him, the endless nights they shared together,
dancing in the sticky hot air,
holding each other like something that could shatter.

I think of her pink fingertips,
how that must have been the sign,
how they must have looked at her blush hands,
and seen only him.
Only her lover, only the mark of their time together.
How Demeter must have seen her hands
and thought only of the stain,
of how her daughter left, a girl, and returned soiled,
just another filthy sheet to be washed in the village.
I think of how tired Persephone must have been,
of all the walking, of trying to please both sides of herself,
of trying to live in between the darkness and the light.

As I finish my pinching and pushing and pulling,
I am so tired I can think only of the pomegranate.
Of the taste of its seeds. Of breaking open each morsel
and crushing it between my teeth.

Far away I can hear the washerwomen, the community,
Persephone. They tell me in chorus,
we are tired too; do what we could not.

And I bite into the flesh with my teeth
and tear the seeds from their snug beds.
I gnash them with my tongue,
lick the sweetness from my lips,
and through my blood red smile,
the chorus in my mind lets out a sigh,
of relief.

An Ode to Things that Make Me Proud to be Fat

I cannot tell you what it is to move as a fat girl,
any more than the ocean can.

When the typhoon stares down the barrel of the shore,
spews at spits and fills the air with its brine,
daring for someone to fight it for space,
to insist it doesn't belong here in this place
where it lived before there was anything else;

and how can I tell you about fighting for space
without telling you about monsoon season in Arizona.
The way summer begins on the heels of winter.
The way the cracked and dry desert sand
splits open like a chasm.
The way the rain breaks through the sky in a blink.
There is no warning,
no sprinkle or cool wind,
only the shout of thunder
before the shower.
Then the chasm is filled,
the green deepens to emerald,
and all at once it is gone again.
It only came to remind the grown of its taste,
to tease the graves with life.

And how can I talk about life as a fat girl,
without pointing to my grandmother's grapefruit tree
sinking under the weight of heavy and ripe bulbs.
How the tree will be more pink than green.
We will wait until the branches
are brushing the dirt beneath them
before plucking the treasure
with our bare hands.
This harvest will all but fall into our palms,
eager to fill our bellies,
to water our throats with its sour-sweet juice.

I cannot tell you about the eagerness to fill
without also telling you about the moon,
full and shining each month, sitting on the horizon.
How we nearly forget it is there until it slips into view,
forces us to stare in awe and remember
how much control it really has.

And the meteor showers, those distracting show offs,
how easy it is to gain attention as a fat girl.
Everyone is already staring,
everyone is already looking at the open dark sky of you
so, if you have their attention,
you might as well wow them.

I want to tell you what a gift it is
to be the fat girl in the room;
how exciting it is to know
you garner the most attention.

That you are the sunrise over the river,
you are the mountains in the middle of the valley,
you are the single source of water in the desert,
even when they hate you,
they need you to stay alive.

P.S.

I don't remember the exact day, maybe it was Summer.
In my late twenties I realized I still had no idea how to grieve.
I knew what everyone said, the five stages,
which were originally intended for people coming to terms
with being diagnosed with terminal illnesses.
I read all of the books.
I could tell you the songs and words of poets
I thought were the answer. But, in practice,
I had learned where to start.

If you need to start with a joke, start with a joke.
If you need to start with silence,
turn off all of the lights in your room but one.
What I know about grief now is
that no one actually knows how to do it.
Some people are quiet, they isolate,
some are angry and loud,
some eat and some starve.
Until one day, maybe in the Summer,
they realize they've been carried on in their lives
the whole time.

The work you just read was what I learned
between my Spring and Summer,
a season that lasted years.
The collection of death, grief, life and love are put together
because I do not know how to have one without the other.

In the pages behind you, you meet people I know,
and the people I don't know,
and the people I surround myself with most,
the characters from television.

I hope these small pieces of myself I've given to you
give you some understanding of how messy grief really is.
I cannot have grief without death
and I cannot have death without fear.

Your tangle may look different than mine,
the world you move through is different than mine,
and it is my hope that your brief look into my life
can help bring some clarity to your own.

Author— Profile:

Carly Herriges is a writer from Tucson, Arizona. She graduated in 2018 from Falmouth University with a degree in Journalism and Creative Writing. In her free time she enjoys reading books on her endless "to be read" list, watching far too much television, and singing karaoke with friends. This is her second poetry collection.

www.ingramcontent.com/pod-product-compliance
Lightning Source LLC
Chambersburg PA
CBHW072103110526
44590CB00018B/3293